Deloitte.

Deloitte & Touche, LLP

Final Report for

Food and Drug Administration

Evaluation of the Adjustment for Changes in Review Activities Applied to the Prescription Drug User Fee Act (PDUFA) IV Workload Adjuster for FY 2009

March 31, 2009

Contract No. GS 32F-8132H,
Order No. HHSF223200830330G.

Deloitte.

Table of Contents

Food and Drug Administration

Draft

Evaluation of the Adjustment for Changes in Review Activities

Applied to the Prescription Drug User Fee Act (PDUFA) IV

Workload Adjuster for FY 2009

1.   Background

The *Prescription Drug User Fee Act* (PDUFA) authorizes the Food and Drug Administration (FDA) to collect user fees for reviewing and processing applications for the approval of certain human drug and biological products. There are generally four types of applications reviewed: *New Drug Applications/Biologics License Applications* (NDAs/BLAs); *Investigational New Drug Applications* (INDs); *Efficacy Supplements*; and *Manufacturing Supplements*.[1] More information on the Prescription Drug User Fee Act can be found at the following website: http://www.fda.gov/ForIndustry/UserFees/PrescriptionDrugUserFee/default.htm.

The Prescription Drug User Fee Amendments of 2002 (known as PDUFA III) provided that after user fees were adjusted for inflation; they should be further adjusted to reflect changes in workload associated with review processes of human drug applications. Congressional reports accompanying PDUFA III outlined a methodology for the PDUFA III Workload Adjuster to capture such changes in workload. The Workload Adjuster was utilized to measure changes in workload demand for reviewing drug and biologic applications during Fiscal Year (FY) 2003 through FY 2007. According to FDA and industry[2], and the action taken by Congress in enacting PDUFA IV, the PDUFA III Workload Adjuster was found to be flawed for NDA/BLA and IND applications in two ways:

---

[1] The Federal Food, Drug, and Cosmetic Act (the act), as amended by the Prescription Drug User Fee Amendments of 2007 (Title 1 of the Food and Drug Administration Amendments Act of 2007 (FDAAA)) (PDUFA IV), authorizes FDA to collect user fees for certain applications for approval of drug and biological products, on establishments where the products are made, and on such products. (http://frwebgate.access.gpo.gov/cgi-bin/getdoc.cgi?dbname=2007_register&docid=fr12oc07-64)

[2] Federal Register Notice / Vol. 72, No. 9 / Tuesday, January 16, 2007/Section II.A.2.b. The FDA published proposed recommendations for the reauthorization of the Prescription Drug User Fee program for the process of human drug application review for FY 2008 to 2012.
(http://frwebgate.access.gpo.gov/cgi-bin/getdoc.cgi?dbname=2007_register&docid=fr16ja07-60.pdf)

- The surrogate for IND workload was the number of new commercial INDs submitted each year. Since each IND application is active for several years, the number of new IND applications submitted in any given year was determined to be a poor surrogate for total IND workload.

- The Workload Adjuster did not take into account some significant factors which increased workload required to review an application. During the PDUFA III time period, there was a substantial increase in the numbers of meetings scheduled[3] and *Special Protocol Assessments* (SPAs) per IND submission. However, the PDUFA III Workload Adjuster only considered changes in the numbers of IND submissions and not the additional review activity required for each application submitted.

As part of the scheduled reauthorization of PDUFA III in FY 2007, Congress remedied the deficiencies arising from the implementation of PDUFA III Workload Adjuster in the PDUFA IV Workload Adjuster with adjustments for changes in review activities, which covers FY 2008 through FY 2012, in the following ways:

- The PDUFA IV Workload Adjuster changed the surrogate for IND workload in the statute from the number of new commercial INDs received each year to the total number of commercial INDs that were active each year. Active IND applications are those that have additional data submitted at least once in the previous 12 months.

- Adjustments for changes in review activities will be applied to the number of new NDA/BLA applications and active INDs each FY. The PDUFA IV workload model adjusts these numbers in proportion to the impact of select review activities that fall under each application type. For NDAs/BLAs, adjustments for changes in review activities are based upon the *number of NDA/BLA meetings scheduled, labeling supplements* and *annual reports*. For INDs, the adjustments for changes in review activities are based upon the *number of IND meetings scheduled* and *SPAs*.

- PDUFA IV specifies that the Secretary shall contract with an independent accounting firm to study the adjustment for changes in review activity applied in setting fees and revenue amounts for FY 2009, and to make changes in the methodology for calculating changes in review activities in future years, if warranted.

2. Objectives and Scope of the Study

FDA engaged Deloitte to conduct an evaluation of the *adjustment for changes in review activities* applied to the PDUFA IV Workload Adjuster for setting PDUFA user fees for FY

---

[3] The FDA collects data on the number of meetings scheduled, requested, held, and meeting minutes. Data captured by FDA on meetings scheduled accurately reflect the meetings that actually took place for IND and NDA/BLA reviews, based upon Deloitte's discussion with key FDA personnel.

2009, and to make appropriate recommendations for change, if warranted. After considering potential recommendations from the study, FDA may change the workload adjustment methodology for setting fees for FY 2010 through FY 2012.

The objectives of this study are to:

- Assess the validity of the adjustments for changes in review activities within the PDUFA IV Workload Adjuster that are applied in setting fees for FY 2009.

- Make recommendations, if warranted, for future changes to the methodology for calculating the adjustments for changes in review activities, using existing or currently available data collected by FDA.

The scope of this study includes an assessment of the adjustments for future changes in review activities in the PDUFA IV Workload Adjuster. Validation of FDA's standard cost model and review of the design and operation of time reporting systems are beyond the scope of this study.

3.   Project Methodology

Our approach for the evaluation of the adjustments for changes in review activities for the PDUFA IV Workload Adjuster included the performance of the following tasks:

- Discussed with FDA the objectives of this study pertaining to the scope described above.

- Held meetings with the FDA team and center staffs to gain an understanding of the terminology and processes associated with the PDUFA IV Workload Adjuster.

- Obtained information on the methodology and calculations associated with the PDUFA IV Workload Adjuster.

- Made data requests based on currently available data.

- Used data received and knowledge gained through meetings to design alternative models and implement several data analysis techniques in an attempt to make an assessment on the adjustments for changes in review activities.

- Provided observations and suggestions to FDA based on the results of the data analysis and assessment.

- Assisted FDA with understanding our methodologies and analysis techniques and discussed potential recommendations and the viability of their implementation with currently available data.

This report documents the assessment of the adjustments for changes in review activities, as well as the potential modifications to the methodology for calculating the adjustments for changes in review activities.

4.   Work Performed

4.1   Understanding of the FDA Methodology

Figure 1 below shows the PDUFA IV Workload Adjuster (also referred to as the baseline model) with the adjustments for changes in review activities.

Application Type	Column 1 5-Year Avg. Base Years 2002-2007	Column 2a Latest 5-Year Avg. 2003-2008	Column 2b Adjustment for changes in Review Activity	Column 2c is Column 2a increased by Column 2b	Column 3 Percent Change	Column 4 Weighting Factor	Column 5 Weighted % Change
NDA's/BLA's	123.8	128.4	-0.55%	127.7	3.1%	33.3%	1.05%
Active Commercial IND's	5,755.8	5,897.6	0.39%	5,920.6	2.9%	45.2%	1.31%
Efficacy Supps.	163.4	173	NA	173	5.9%	8.3%	0.49%
Manufacturing Supps.	2,589.2	2,616.2	NA	2,616.2	1.0%	13.2%	0.14%
FY 2009 Workload Adjuster With Adjustment for Changes in review Activities							2.98%

Figure 1 – PDUFA IV Workload Adjuster with Adjustments for Changes in Review Activities[4]

Column 1 displays the baseline 5-year averages calculated based on the number of submissions for each application type for the FY 2002 through FY 2007.

Column 2a displays the current 5-year averages calculated based on the number of submissions for each application type for the FY 2003 through FY 2008.

Column 2b displays the percentage change in workload for the NDA/BLA and IND application types, which are also referred to as the *adjustments for changes in review activities.*

Column 2c represents the adjusted current 5-year averages from Column 2a after the adjustments in Column 2b are applied to Column 2a. (Note that only the 5-year averages for the NDA/BLA and IND application types change.)

Column 3 represents the percent change in workload from Column 1 to Column 2c.

Column 4 displays the appropriate weighting factors that are applied to each application type. Background information on how the weighting factors are calculated is summarized as follows:

---

[4]Federal Register/ Volume 73, Number 149, "Food and Drug Administration, Prescription Drug User Fee Rates for Fiscal Year 2009" pg. 45020, Table 4, August 1, 2008. (Column 2c for Efficacy Supplements was changed to reflect 173 and Manufacturing Supplements was changed to reflect 2616.2; Per our evaluation and discussion with the FDA, 173.3 and 2516.2, respectively, were misprinted in the Federal Register.

- The PDUFA IV Workload Adjuster utilizes time reporting data to capture the level of effort utilized during the process for the review of human drug applications. The Center for Drug Evaluation and Research (CDER) and the Center for Biologics Evaluation and Research (CBER) both conduct time reporting surveys to gather information on the level of effort utilized for the process for the review of human drug applications.[5]

- The CDER and CBER time reporting data is also used by FDA in generating estimates of standard costs for the process of human drug review. The standard cost model generates estimates of the average processing costs for each application type.[6] These standard cost estimates are then used to create weighting factors for each application type included in the PDUFA IV Workload Adjuster.

- The weighting factors displayed are also the average weights over the most recent 5-year period.

Column 5 displays the workload adjustment for each application type. These weighted percentages are calculated by multiplying the weighting factor in Column 4 by the percent change in workload in Column 3. The sum of the weighted percentages for each application type shown in Column 5 represents the final adjustment in workload of 2.98% for FY 2009.

---

[5] CDER employs the Time Reporting System (TRS) to collect data on time spent on the four application types listed above. CDER collects information from two four-week periods at two different points during the year, for a total of 8 weeks of data. CBER employs the Resource Reporting System (RRS) to collect data on the time spent on the four applications types (NDA/BLAs, Active Commercial IND's, Efficacy Supplements, and Manufacturing Supplements). CBER collects information from one pay period (two weeks) per quarter, for a total of 8 weeks of data. The distribution of time reported is allocated through FTEs to each of the offices that are directly responsible for reviews. For both centers, the time reported represents the level of effort expended on each review activity based on a set of activity codes put forth by FDA. (These activity codes represent the different types of review activities associated with the process for the review of human drug applications as defined in PDUFA.) Both centers use the time related to the direct review of applications as a driver to allocate the time of the offices that perform functions that indirectly support the process for the review of human drug applications.

[6] The process costs are based on obligation amounts that are obtained from the Office of Financial Management (OFM) and distributed, based on time reporting data, to various application types.

Figure 2 below depicts a flow of the PDUFA IV Workload Adjuster that is shown in Figure 1. The enlarged box with a bolded border represents the adjustments for changes in review activities (Column 2b), which is the specific area of study within the scope of this project.[7]

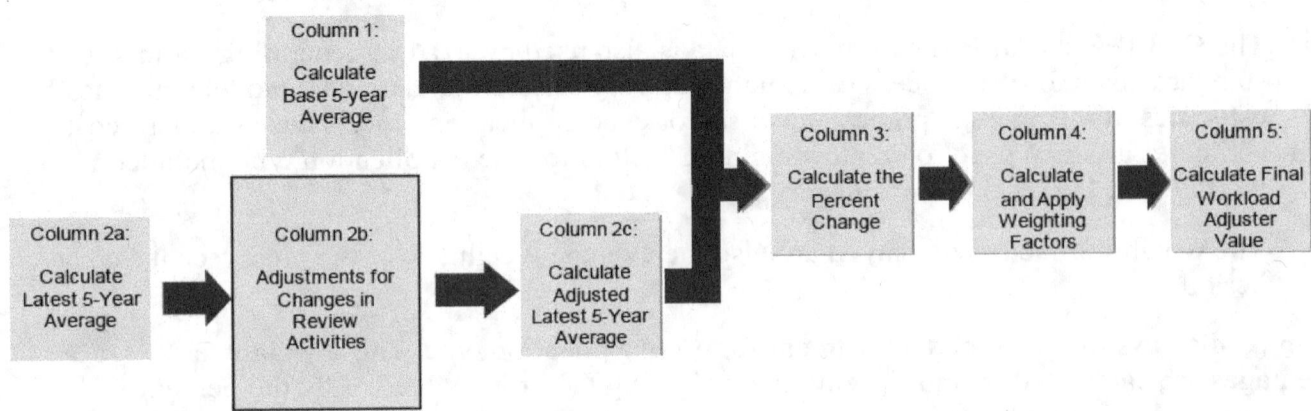

Figure 2 – Flow of PDUFA IV Workload Adjuster with Adjustments for Changes in Review Activities

Based on our understanding of the FDA methodology for the PDUFA IV Workload Adjuster with adjustments for changes in review activities, five specific review activities were identified by FDA as the primary drivers contributing to observed increases in the application review workload over the years. These specific review activities are not an exhaustive list of application-review related activities; however they are able to be measured in terms of relative level of effort. The additional work necessary to perform these specific review activities was not captured in the PDUFA III Workload Adjuster. The five review activities and the associated application types are:

New Drug Applications (NDAs) / Biologics License Applications (BLAs)

1. Labeling Supplements: The FDA reviews the labeling supplements for human prescription drug and biological products to assess pertinent information about the appropriate use of drugs.

2. Annual Reports: The review of annual reports submitted for NDAs/BLAs from sponsors on an annual basis.[8]

3. NDA/BLA Meetings Scheduled: Meetings scheduled during the review of NDAs/BLAs.

---

[7] A more detailed diagram illustrating our understanding of the PDUFA IV Workload Adjuster is included in Appendix A.

[8] Annual reports for Abbreviated New Drug Applications (ANDAs) were not included in the PDUFA IV Workload Adjuster with adjustments for changes in review activities.

Investigational New Drug (IND) Applications

4. Special Protocol Assessments (SPAs): The FDA reviews the SPAs submitted by sponsors to assess whether they are adequate to meet scientific and regulatory requirements identified by the sponsors. Three types of protocols related to PDUFA products are eligible for this special protocol assessment under the PDUFA goals: Animal Carcinogenicity protocols; Final Product Stability protocols; and Clinical protocols.

5. IND Meetings Scheduled: Meetings scheduled during the review of IND applications.

The adjustments for changes in review activities (Column 2b in Figure 1) were calculated by first calculating the individual *activity factors* for each of the review activities listed above. The activity factor is a product of the *percent change in level of effort* and the *average time weighting factor*. Once the activity factor was calculated for each individual review activity component, the percentages were totaled by application type to derive the final *adjustments for changes in review activities*, as percentages. The details of the calculation are described below:

*   Step 1: To obtain the *percent change in level of effort* for each review activity component, the current and base 5-year average counts for the review activity were divided by the current and base 5-year average submission counts for the corresponding application type. For example, the most recent 5-year average number of Labeling Supplements was divided by the most recent 5-year average number of new NDA/BLA submissions; the most recent 5-year average number of SPAs was divided by the most recent 5-year average number of Active INDs. Next, the percentage change for the current year was calculated relative to the base year, for each review activity component.

*   Step 2: To obtain the *average time weighting factor* for each review activity component, the percent of CDER and CBER time spent on each review activity was multiplied by the percent of total CDER and CBER time spent on the corresponding application type, for each fiscal year. For example, ([% of CDER time spent on Labeling Supplements] x [% of total CDER NDA/BLA time]) + [% of CBER time spent on Labeling Supplements] x [% of total CBER NDA/BLA time]) = Time Weighting Factor for Labeling Supplements (as a percentage). The average time weighting factor for the current year was calculated by computing the average value for each review activity component for the most recent 5-year period.

*   Step 3: The percentages resulting from Step 1 and Step 2 were multiplied to produce the final activity factor for each review activity component.

*   Step 4: The activity factors for Labeling Supplements (-0.09%), Annual Reports (-0.07%), and NDA/BLA Meetings Scheduled (-0.39%) were added together to generate the total -0.55% adjustment for changes in review activities for NDAs/BLAs. The activity factors for SPAs (0.09%) and IND Meetings Scheduled (0.30%) were added together to generate the total 0.39% adjustment for changes in review activities for INDs.

The remainder of this report discusses the evaluation, study, and assessment of these adjustments for changes in review activities.

4.2   Evaluation and Study

4.2.1   Assumptions

Deloitte's evaluation and study is based on the following assumptions.

1. The information and data obtained from the FDA Project Officer and other FDA key team members are accurate and complete.[9]

2. Operational data collected from CDER and CBER's time reporting systems are adequate for capturing the human drug application review activities (e.g., number of SPAs, NDA/BLA meetings scheduled, annual reports, etc.).

3. The eight-week samples used for CDER and CBER time reporting surveys are considered to be representative of the level of effort for application review-related activities for the entire year.

4. Time reported using activity codes in the time reporting survey adequately reflect the actual application review activities associated with the level of effort expended by CDER and CBER.

5. The percentage distributions of CDER and CBER time reported for each office in the standard cost model are valid and accurate.

6. The methodology for developing relative weights based on standard costs is appropriate.

7. Since pay and benefit costs represent the majority of the CDER and CBER expenses, the obligation amounts used in the standard cost model are a close representation of the actual total CDER and CBER expenses.

8. According to FDA, the non-labor obligations are proportional to labor obligations. Therefore, FDA's use of total obligations in the standard cost model to represent the process costs of the PDUFA-related activities is appropriate.

9. The PDUFA IV Workload Adjuster and the adjustment for changes in review activities are unique. Currently, there is no authoritative guidance, existing metric, historical data, or other similar methodology available for measuring its effectiveness.

4.2.2   Data Collection and Validation

Data validation efforts associated with the adjustments for changes in review activities involved comparing the PDUFA IV Workload Adjuster data with the data provided from CDER and CBER for the following seven data elements: 1) Labeling Supplements; 2) Annual Reports; 3)

---

[9] Deloitte performed within scope validation work (see Section 4.2.2).

NDA/BLA Meetings Scheduled; 4) NDA/BLA Applications; 5) SPAs; 6) IND Meetings Scheduled and 7) IND Applications. The data provided by CDER and CBER included submission counts for NDAs/BLAs and INDs for PDUFA years 2002 through 2008. CDER and CBER also provided activity factor counts for the five review activities mentioned above for PDUFA years 2002 through 2008. The CDER and CBER time reporting data for FY 2006 through FY 2008 was deemed out of scope of this evaluation due to the sensitive nature of the data.

Data requests were submitted to CDER and CBER to obtain the counts associated with the seven data elements. The data was obtained by each center from the systems where the information is stored. The data validation efforts are summarized in Figure 3 below for each column in the PDUFA IV Workload Adjuster.

Column	Data Element	Data Validation
1	Submission Counts: - Labeling Supplements - Annual Reports - NDA/BLA Meetings Scheduled - NDA/BLA Applications - SPAs - IND Meetings Scheduled - IND Applications	Validated against data received from CDER and CBER
2a	Submission Counts: - Labeling Supplements - Annual Reports - NDA/BLA Meetings Scheduled - NDA/BLA Applications - SPAs - IND Meetings Scheduled - IND Applications	
2b	Activity Factor Data: - Labeling Supplements - Annual Reports - NDA/BLA Meetings Scheduled - SPAs - IND Meetings Scheduled	
2c	Derived from Columns 2a and 2b	Not Applicable
3	Derived from Columns 1 and 2c	Not Applicable
4	Weighting Factors: - NDAs/BLAs - INDs	Validated against weighting factors obtained from the Standard Cost Model. The Standard Cost model is beyond the scope of this project, therefore no validation is performed on any of the Standard Cost Model data
5	Derived from Columns 3 and 4	Not Applicable

Figure 3 – Summary of Data Validation Efforts for the PDUFA IV Workload Adjuster

The results of the data validation for each of the seven data elements are shown in the tables below (Figures 4 through 10), and is followed by an explanation of any variances found.

Labeling Supplements					
PDUFA Year	CDER Data [a]	CBER Data [b]	Total CDER & CBER [a] + [b] = [c]	PDUFA IV Workload Adjuster [d]	Variance [c] - [d] = [e]	Percentage Difference [e] / [c] = [f]
2002	761	74	835	815	20	2.40%
2003	773	93	866	836	30	3.46%
2004	1,011	70	1,081	1,040	41	3.79%
2005	776	50	826	787	39	4.72%
2006	885	49	934	902	32	3.43%
2007	1,024	53	1,077	1,037	40	3.71%
2008	912	48	960	914	46	4.79%

Figure 4 – Data Validation Results for Labeling Supplements

Annual Reports					
PDUFA Year	CDER Data [a]	CBER Data [b]	Total CDER & CBER [a] + [b] = [c]	PDUFA IV Workload Adjuster [d]	Variance [c] - [d] = [e]	Percentage Difference [e] / [c] = [f]
2002	2,672	226	2,898	2,897	1	0.03%
2003	2,651	275	2,926	2,925	1	0.03%
2004	2,575	187	2,762	2,761	1	0.04%
2005	2,651	158	2,809	2,808	1	0.04%
2006	2,581	191	2,772	2,771	1	0.04%
2007	2,676	194	2,870	2,868	2	0.07%
2008	2,672	222	2,894	2,891	3	0.10%

Figure 5 – Data Validation Results for Annual Reports

NDA/BLA Meetings Scheduled					
PDUFA Year	CDER Data [a]	CBER Data [b]	Total CDER & CBER [a] + [b] = [c]	PDUFA IV Workload Adjuster [d]	Variance [c] - [d] = [e]	Percentage Difference [e] / [c] = [f]
2002	342	74	416	416	0	0.00%
2003	412	80	492	492	0	0.00%
2004	366	55	421	399	22	5.23%
2005	328	42	370	346	24	6.49%
2006	328	58	386	372	14	3.63%
2007	285	44	329	316	13	3.95%
2008	238	62	300	296	4	1.33%

Figure 6 – Data Validation Results for NDA/BLA Meetings Scheduled

PDUFA Year	CDER Data [a]	CBER Data [b]	Total CDER & CBER [a] + [b] = [c]	PDUFA IV Workload Adjuster [d]	Variance [c] - [d] = [e]	Percentage Difference [e] / [c] = [f]
NDA/BLA Applications						
2002	90	9	99	99	0	0.00%
2003	113	8	121	115	6	4.96%
2004	129	6	135	138	-3	-2.22%
2005	105	9	114	117	-3	-2.63%
2006	128	4	132	133	-1	-0.76%
2007	109	15	124	116	8	6.45%
2008	141	4	145	138	7	4.83%

Figure 7 – Data Validation Results for NDA/BLA Applications

PDUFA Year	CDER Data [a]	CBER Data [b]	Total CDER & CBER [a] + [b] = [c]	PDUFA IV Workload Adjuster [d]	Variance [c] - [d] = [e]	Percentage Difference [e] / [c] = [f]
SPAs						
2002	204	0	204	206	-2	-0.98%
2003	295	17	312	314	-2	-0.64%
2004	329	13	342	341	1	0.29%
2005	384	10	394	397	-3	-0.76%
2006	423	12	435	437	-2	-0.46%
2007	421	11	432	433	-1	-0.23%
2008	387	10	397	403	-6	-1.51%

Figure 8 – Data Validation Results for SPAs

PDUFA Year	CDER Data [a]	CBER Data [b]	Total CDER & CBER [a] + [b] = [c]	PDUFA IV Workload Adjuster [d]	Variance [c] - [d] = [e]	Percentage Difference [e] / [c] = [f]
IND Meetings Scheduled						
2002	758	283	1,041	1,040	1	0.10%
2003	1,016	316	1,332	1,338	-6	-0.45%
2004	1,338	196	1,534	1,537	-3	-0.20%
2005	1,649	196	1,845	1,819	26	1.41%
2006	1,733	200	1,933	1,942	-9	-0.47%
2007	1,670	191	1,861	1,861	0	0.00%
2008	1,533	210	1,743	1,767	-24	-1.38%

Figure 9 – Data Validation Results for IND Meetings Scheduled

PDUFA Year	CDER Data [a]	CBER Data [b]	Total CDER & CBER [a] + [b] = [c]	PDUFA IV Workload Adjuster [d]	Variance [c] - [d] = [e]	Percentage Difference [e] / [c] = [f]
2002	3,659	1,320	4,979	4,982	-3	-0.06%
2003	3,764	1,352	5,116	5,123	-7	-0.14%
2004	4,766	888	5,654	5,661	-7	-0.12%
2005	5,047	843	5,890	5,900	-10	-0.17%
2006	5,385	829	6,214	6,252	-38	-0.61%
2007	5,168	824	5,992	5,843	149	2.49%
2008	5,521	864	6,385	5,832	553	8.66%

Figure 10 – Data Validation Results for IND Applications

According to the FDA, the discrepancies found between values that were used in the PDUFA IV Workload Adjuster and the values provided to us by the FDA for verification purposes were due to querying the source databases at different points in time. Variances may occur in the data because of the dynamic nature of the source data and constant updates to the data. Properties and attributes of a given application may be adjusted as necessary during the course of a review and any updates to that application are then made within the system accordingly. Examples affecting submission counts and complexity factors may include:

- **Data Entry Lag:** It may take a few days from the receipt of an application to its entry into the database. If the database is queried by a user during this window, the results of the query may underestimate the total submission count for that application type. For example, if three new submissions are received on June 30th (the cut-off date for the PDUFA year used in the Workload Adjuster), they may not be captured in a query that is run immediately after that date. FDA analysts try to mitigate this risk by deferring the database query until the last possible moment.
- **Data Update Lag:** Since individual application submissions include many fields that need to be accurately flagged, these critical flags may not be known until substantial review of the submission package has been performed; this process can take up to two months (for example, an NDA needs to be categorized as a New Molecular Entity (NME) or a non-NME, and also as to whether or not it includes clinical data). Even after adding flags there may be some time before FDA has time to update the submission in the system because of competing priorities. If the database is queried while these submissions are being processed, the results of the query may not represent the final number of submissions until all entries have been updated. It is important to note that the data update lag will affect the NDA/BLA sub-types but it will not have a significant impact on the overall count.
- **FDA Data Reporting Method:** Under the current methodology for collecting and reporting the data used in the PDUFA workload adjuster, the data is collected for each 12 month period ending on June 30th, and recorded in mid July. To make periods from earlier years comparable with later years, the amounts from earlier years are not restated - they always remain fixed at the values initially reported for each year. Naturally, restating

these values for purposes of our evaluation produced values that generally differed slightly from the values initially recorded and repeated here without change for the associated year.

- **Human Entry Errors:** Errors may occur by the user when the application is entered into the system or updated. Multiple levels of quality assurance are performed on a frequent basis, but resource constraints make this difficult at times.

- **New Data Systems:** During the past few years, FDA's CDER has been moving towards a new consolidated database for submission types, namely, the Document Archiving, Reporting, and Regulatory Tracking System (DARRTS). CDER IND applications were moved to DARRTS in 2007 and CDER NDA applications are planned for migration in 2009. This new database features a greater reliance on automated updates to data based on clearly defined business rules which reduces the need for manual data entry (which would help minimize data entry and update lags as well as human entry errors). This database also includes a robust trace-back feature that will document changes made to the database. However, moving to a new database does introduce several issues that may affect the stability of the data:

  o When data are migrated from one system to another, there is a possibility that data may be lost or altered during the move. FDA exercises extensive quality assurance measures to maintain data integrity during the migration.

  o Any new database structure will also require the development of new queries that would provide the same results that were obtained from the older database. FDA has experienced challenges building comparable queries using the new Business Object query interface. Training is being provided to support the development of queries capable of navigating the intricacies of the data being queried. Until all data migration issues have been addressed, some variability in the query results will be expected.

We performed a simulation analysis of the adjustments for changes in review activities for the PDUFA IV Workload Adjuster by utilizing the data received in support of our validation effort (see the 2nd, 3rd and 4th columns of figures 4-10) as new inputs. Based on the results of the simulations we believe that the data variances do not represent a significant impact to the adjustments for changes in review activities. However, we believe that FDA could implement additional procedures to reduce these data variances (see observations section below).

4.2.3   Approach and Results

We addressed the assessment of the adjustment for changes in review activities for the PDUFA IV Workload Adjuster from three different perspectives. The first approach yielded an alternative model to allow for a comparative analysis to the baseline model described above. The second approach, the sensitivity analysis, was intended to generate alternative models that would serve as a basis for comparison to the baseline model. However, due to certain limitations described in the section that follows, we were unable to proceed with the sensitivity analysis approach. The third approach, the Monte Carlo Analysis, yielded results for both the baseline and the alternative models that served as a basis to provide meaningful insight on the reasonableness of the adjustments for changes in review activities.

The following section provides more detail regarding the three approaches outlined above.

Developing an Alternative Model

The alternative model was designed by considering three modifications to the current PDUFA IV adjustments for changes in review activity. These three modifications directly impact the calculations involved with the adjustments for changes in review activities. These modifications may enhance the current Workload Adjuster's ability to measure the change in workload.

The first modification involved adding another review activity for the NDA/BLA applications. This additional activity captured the change in workload associated with the review of NDA/BLA Resubmissions since this activity could have a potentially significant impact on the workload. The activity factor for this review activity was computed using the same methodology that was used to calculate the five original application activity factors. However, discussions with the FDA team revealed this to be an imprudent modification due to the fact that FDA currently has multiple initiatives in place designed to achieve a higher percentage of first cycle review decisions and correspondingly reducing the number of application resubmissions. Inherent in this FDA initiative to increase the number of first-cycle decisions is an increase in the relative work and staff time spent during the initial review cycle. Therefore, the number of NDA/BLA resubmissions was expected to decline and as a result, not be relevant to the adjustments for changes in review activities. Consequently, this modification was excluded from the analysis.

The second modification involved excluding the denominator when calculating the activity factors for each of the five application review activities. The two denominators reflect the number of new NDA/BLA applications and the number of IND applications with activity. Excluding these two denominators in the calculations would avoid a risk of underestimating changes in workload by removing potential double-counting of submissions and further scaling down the year-to-year percent changes. It is important to mention that the workload has increased on a per-submission basis due to the increasing complexity of the applications received; however, an in-depth review led us to realize that certain review activities are not as directly related to the two denominators as other activities. For example, Annual Reports are largely independent of the number of new NDAs/BLAs received; whereas the number of NDA/BLA Meetings Scheduled is slightly more dependent on the number of new NDAs/BLAs received. Including a different NDA/BLA denominator in the calculation of the activity factors for both of these review activities would have potentially provided a better estimate of the relative change in workload. The ideal modification would involve excluding the denominator for some review activities and not others to avoid a double-counting of submissions. However, executing this modification with the existing calculations would have led to some review activities having a large activity factor percentage and other review activities having a small activity factor percentage. When totaled, those disproportionate activity factors (very large percentages and very small percentages) would have misrepresented the actual change in workload. As a result, a decision was made to exclude this modification from the alternative model as well.

The third modification involved weighting the time reporting percentages that were used to calculate each activity factor. The reason for applying weights to the time reporting percentages was because the existing 5-year time reporting averages (also used in the calculation) implicitly assume that the time reporting percentages are relative to each other on a yearly basis, which would result in accurately capturing workload changes. However, due to increases in FDA staff levels over time, the 5-year time reporting averages were only capturing average time spent in a particular year. Therefore, the time reporting weighting factors were generated based on *average* time spent year-to-year and fail to reflect *relative* time spent year-to-year. The proposed modification used weighted process costs to generate new time reporting weighting factors that were based on relative year-to-year changes for each review activity component. (The process costs for NDAs/BLAs and INDs, for FY 2006 through FY 2008, were obtained from the standard cost model.) The new weighting factors were then used in the remainder of the calculation that produced the new adjustments for changes in review activities for NDAs/BLAs and INDs. The new adjustments for changes in review activities were used to develop another Workload Adjuster (alternative model), shown in Figure 11 below. The specific modifications made to the existing calculations are included in Appendix D.

Application Type	Column 1 5-Year Avg. Base Years 2002-2007	Column 2a Latest 5-Year Avg. 2003-2008	Column 2b Adjustment for changes in Review Activity	Column 2c is Column 2a increased by Column 2b	Column 3 Percent Change	Column 4 Weighting Factor	Column 5 Weighted % Change
NDA's/BLA's	123.8	128.4	-0.46%	127.8	3.2%	33.3%	1.08%
Active Commercial IND's	5,755.8	5,897.6	0.39%	5,920.6	2.9%	45.2%	1.29%
Efficacy Supps.	163.4	173	*NA*	173	5.9%	8.3%	0.49%
Manufacturing Supps.	2,589.2	2,616.2	*NA*	2,616.2	1.0%	13.2%	0.14%
FY 2009 Workload Adjuster With Adjustment for Changes in review Activities							3.00%

Figure 11 – Alternative Model[10]

The adjustments for changes in review activities for NDAs/BLAs changed slightly from -0.55% in the baseline model to -0.46% in the alternative model. However, for INDs, the adjustment for changes in review activities remained the same for both models, with the percentage being 0.39%. The alternative model yielded a final Workload Adjuster value of 3.00%.

The alternative model was also subject to the Monte Carlo analysis technique, which is described at the end of this section.

Sensitivity Analysis

A Sensitivity Analysis technique was intended to modify the Workload Adjuster inputs (the level of effort for each of the activity factors) to achieve a reasonable range of values for the final adjustment in workload. Evaluating this range of outputs would help determine whether or not the adjustments for changes in review activities were capturing the changes in workload. The inputs for the baseline model would have been treated as control data while the level of effort for

---

[10] Federal Register/ Volume 73, Number 149, "Food and Drug Administration, Prescription Drug User Fee Rates for Fiscal Year 2009" pg. 45020, Table 4, August 1, 2008. The values in Column 2b were changed from the original table in Figure 1 based on the modifications described for the alternative model.

each review activity would have been increased or decreased through a series of tests. The series of tests would have varied across univariate, bivariate and multivariate analysis. The results of this analysis would have been compared to feedback received from experienced FDA CDER and CBER personnel regarding hypothetical changes in the PDUFA-related workload. This comparison would have created a set of metrics to be used in making a final assessment on the reasonableness of the adjustments for changes in review activities. After discussing this approach with the FDA Project Officer and other key FDA team members, a decision was made not to proceed with this approach due to the lack of time available for FDA application review staff to respond to the questions due to application review workload demands.

Monte Carlo Analysis

The Monte Carlo methods are a class of computational algorithms that rely on repeated random sampling to generate results.[11] These methods are often used when simulating physical and mathematical systems. In general, Monte Carlo methods are useful for modeling phenomena with significant uncertainty in their inputs. Because of the reliance on repeated computation and the generation of random or pseudo-random numbers, Monte Carlo methods are suited to calculation by a computer. These methods tend to be used when it is infeasible or impossible to compute an exact result with a deterministic algorithm.[12][13] There is no single Monte Carlo method; instead, the term describes a large and widely-used class of approaches. However, these approaches tend to follow a particular pattern as described below:

1. Define a domain of possible inputs to the model as random variables.

2. Generate model inputs from the domain, and use those inputs with the model to perform a deterministic computation.

3. Aggregate the results of a collection (large sample) of individual computations into the final result.

For the evaluation and study of the PDUFA IV Workload Adjuster, the Monte Carlo analysis could potentially add meaningful insight to the behavior of the model. We realize the limitations of this analysis given the limited number of years that the data is provided in the PDUFA IV Workload Adjuster, however, after discussing this approach with the FDA Project Officer and other key FDA team members, this approach was considered as possibly yielding value-added results that could be used for a final assessment. The Monte Carlo analysis was performed as

---

[11] The term Monte Carlo method was coined in the 1940s by physicists working on nuclear weapon projects in the Los Alamos National Laboratory. See the following document for more information: http://library.lanl.gov/la-pubs/00326866.pdf.

[12] Douglas Hubbard "How to Measure Anything: Finding the Value of Intangibles in Business" pg. 46, John Wiley & Sons, 2007

[13] A deterministic algorithm is an algorithm which, in general terms, uses known inputs to calculate or produce a result that can be viewed with a known degree of precision or accuracy.

described in the three steps above for the adjustments for changes in review activities. More specifically, the calculations for the five activity factors were subject to these techniques.

The first step of the Monte Carlo method was to define the domain for each input to the model as random variables. For example, one domain would be the collection of Labeling Supplements that are presented to FDA for review during FY 2008. This domain would then be defined by three parameters: the mean (average), the standard deviation, and the probability distribution function (e.g., normal, "bell curve").

A random number generator in Excel was used to provide inputs to the random variables within the domain. When this process was repeated numerous times (e.g., 500, 1,000 or over 10,000 times) for a properly defined set of random variables, the behavior of the model was observed based on the outputs that were produced.[14] In this study, the varying outputs of the analysis were the overall adjustments in workload (2.98% in the PDUFA IV Workload Adjuster).

The second step of the Monte Carlo method was to generate inputs from each domain for multiple simulations. This was accomplished using a random number generator for the seven model inputs associated with the five review activities and two application types (see Section 4.1).[15] The seven model inputs were Labeling Supplements; Annual Reports; NDA/BLA Meetings Scheduled; NDA/BLA Applications; SPAs; IND Meetings Scheduled; and IND Applications with activity. Each model input had seven data points associated with it (the 5-year averages from FY 2002 through FY 2007). The random variables for each of the model inputs were defined as the differences between the data point and the linear fit for the data (obtained from a regression analysis). The statistical properties of each random variable were described by the mean, standard deviation and a probability distribution function for each variable. The concept for random variables is depicted in Figure 12 below.

---

[14] The ability of the mean, standard deviation and probability distribution function to accurately describe the domain of a random variable is highly dependent on the quantity and quality of data available for each domain. In other words, the more data collected for each domain, the more accurately the Monte Carlo methods can be used to describe the impact of the output.

[15] Since the raw time reporting data was not available for review, it was decided not to perform the Monte Carlo analysis on the time reporting percentages that are also involved in deriving the -0.59% for NDA/BLAs and 0.39% for INDs.

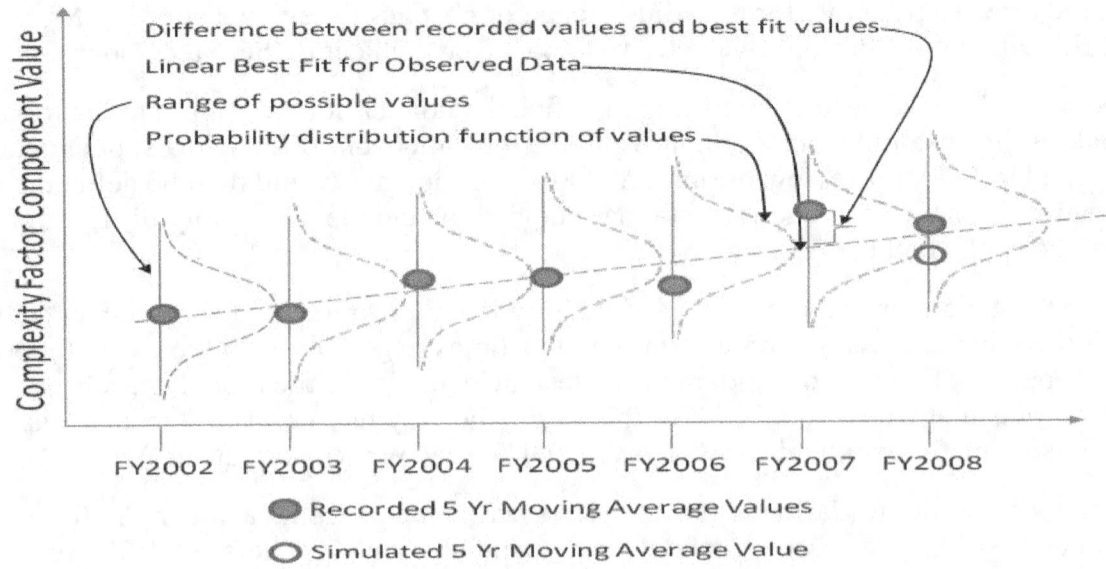

Figure 12 – Random Variables for Each Model Input

The simulated value in Figure 12 represents the FY 2008 value of each of the seven model inputs. The value was generated by first determining the formula for the linear fit through the data points. Since there is a degree of randomness associated with the value of each input, a random error was also added to the linear fit.[16]

The third step of the Monte Carlo method was to aggregate the results of a group of individual Monte Carlo simulations. These results provided a set of statistics which describe the behavior of the various review activities involved with the adjustments for changes in review activities. These statistics were used to evaluate the adjustments for changes in review activities across a reasonable range of values.

The Monte Carlo analysis was applied to the PDUFA IV Workload Adjuster (baseline model) as well as the alternative model. The results for both models are discussed below.

---

[16] The random error was defined by determining the mean and standard deviation of the difference between the recorded values and the values associated with the linear fit and assuming that the random error follows the normal "bell curve" distribution. In other words, seven domains were established.

Statistic	Baseline Model	Alternative Model
Observed Mean	3.1137%	3.1125%
Number of Trials	10,000	10,000
Minimum	2.8115%	2.8156%
Maximum	3.4933%	3.3889%
Median	3.1133%	3.1126%
Range	0.6819%	0.5734%
Standard Deviation	0.0766%	0.0768%
Variance	0.0001%	0.0001%

Figure 13 – Results of Monte Carlo Analysis on PDUFA IV Workload Adjuster Using 5-Year Averages

Figure 13 shows a summary of the results of the Monte Carlo analysis for both of the models. Each model was analyzed using the 5-year Average data (FY 2002 through FY 2008) simulated 10,000 times.

The first observation made from the results was that the Monte Carlo analysis generated a mean value of 3.11% for the final adjustment in workload. The output of the baseline model determined by FDA was 2.98%. The second observation is that the weighted time reporting modification used to develop the alternative model had little effect on the final output of the PDUFA IV Workload Adjuster. The Monte Carlo analysis observed that the mean for the alternative model involving weighted time reporting was also 3.11%. The 3.11% observed mean values is based on the assumption that the seven model inputs are normally distributed. Based on our analysis and discussions with key FDA personnel, the 2.98% output in the baseline model and the 3.00% in the alternative model was an expected result due to the reasons outlined below:

- The 5 year moving averages for the number of SPAs and IND meetings per Active IND increased at slower pace than the PDUFA III years.

- The 5-year moving averages for NDA/BLA annual reports and meetings had declined in FY 2008.

- There was an increase in the 5-year moving average of NDA/BLA labeling supplements, but the number of NDA/BLA applications had increased at a faster pace, leading to an additional decline in the workload adjustment reflected from the NDA/BLA review activity components.

- There was a relatively high number of NDAs received in FY 2007. In addition, the number of BLAs received by CBER increased by a factor of nearly 3 over FY 2006 and FY 2007 levels. The increase in the number of these applications was significantly higher relative to the trends found in the other years; thus, leading to a lower adjustment for FY 2008.

This translated in a decline or a slower increase in workload for FY 2008 as opposed to the increasing trend from the review activity components during the PDUFA III years.

Given the assumptions made above, one could conclude that there is a 50% chance that the FY 2009 adjustment in workload will be greater than 3.11%, and a greater than 50% chance that the FY 2009 adjustment in workload will be greater than 2.98% for the baseline model and a greater than a 50% chance that the FY 2009 adjustment will be greater than 3.00% for the alternative model. (The detailed results of the analysis for each model can be found in Appendix B.)

Given the assumptions made in the Monte Carlo analysis described above, we conclude that the adjustment for changes in review activities has a reasonable degree of stability in the scenarios examined.

5.   Observations

As described in section 4.2.3, a potential alternative model was developed by modifying the calculations pertaining to the average time weighting factors used to produce the adjustments for changes in review activities for the PDUFA IV Workload Adjuster. As part of the development of this potential alternative model, we suggest that the calculation of the average time weighting factors for each review activity component include an additional weighting scheme. This weighting scheme might assist in more accurately capturing the effort expended on each review activity on a relative year-to-year basis. Using the currently available data, the weighting scheme for time weighting factors will utilize CDER and CBER process costs for NDAs/BLAs and INDs for each fiscal year. The specific calculations associated with the weighting scheme for the alternative methodology are included in Appendix D.

Since the alternative model yields only a 0.02% increase in the final PDUFA IV Workload Adjuster value, this may not warrant a change in the current Workload Adjuster. However, we also believe that including this additional weighting factor in the future might provide a methodology to measure workload changes more completely in both absolute and relative terms, and suggest that FDA consider the alternative model in the future as more data become available to test it.

In addition, based on our data validation efforts described in section 4.2.2, we recommend that the FDA should consider implementing additional quality control procedures and maintaining documentation on the data obtained for the adjustment for changes in review activities for the PDUFA IV Workload Adjuster. We have been informally advised by the FDA that such steps are being taken.

6.   Summary of Assessment

Our research and understanding of the review activities and the associated calculations for each activity factor related to the adjustments for changes in review activities for the PDUFA IV Workload Adjuster were key in establishing the framework for making our assessment.

The alternative model used process costs for each application type as an additional weighing scheme for the time reporting percentages. This resulted in a 3.00% final adjustment, which is not significantly different from the 2.98% adjustment in the PDUFA IV Workload Adjuster.

In addition, the results of the Monte Carlo analysis for the baseline and alternative model generated a mean value of 3.11% for the final adjustment in workload. This outcome also provided a means to measure the reasonableness of the adjustments for changes in review activities.

Within the boundaries of the assumptions outlined in section 4.2.1, and based on our analysis and the data that was available to us, our assessment of the current PDUFA IV Workload Adjuster finds that it reasonably captures changes in workload for reviewing human drug applications under PDUFA IV.

7.   Appendix A: Diagram of PDUFA IV Workload Adjuster

The next three diagrams represent our understanding of the PDUFA IV Workload Adjuster.

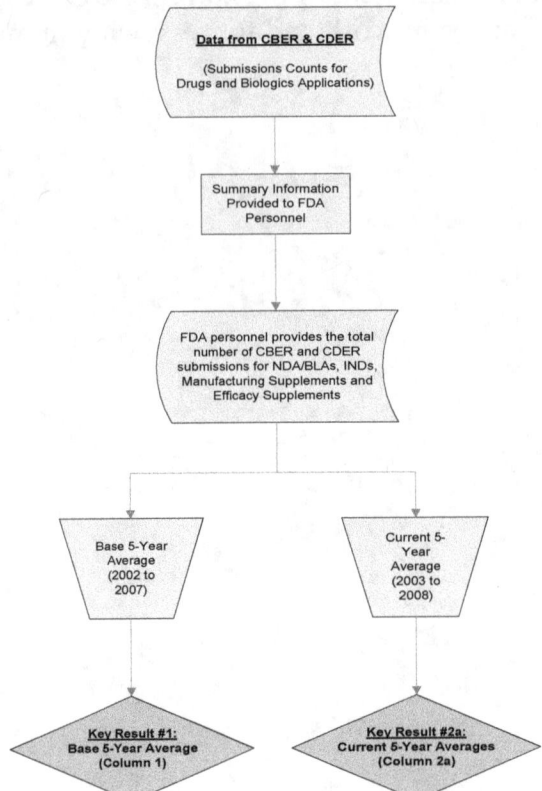

Overview of PDUFA IV Workload Adjuster
Pertaining to the Adjustments for Changes in Review Activities

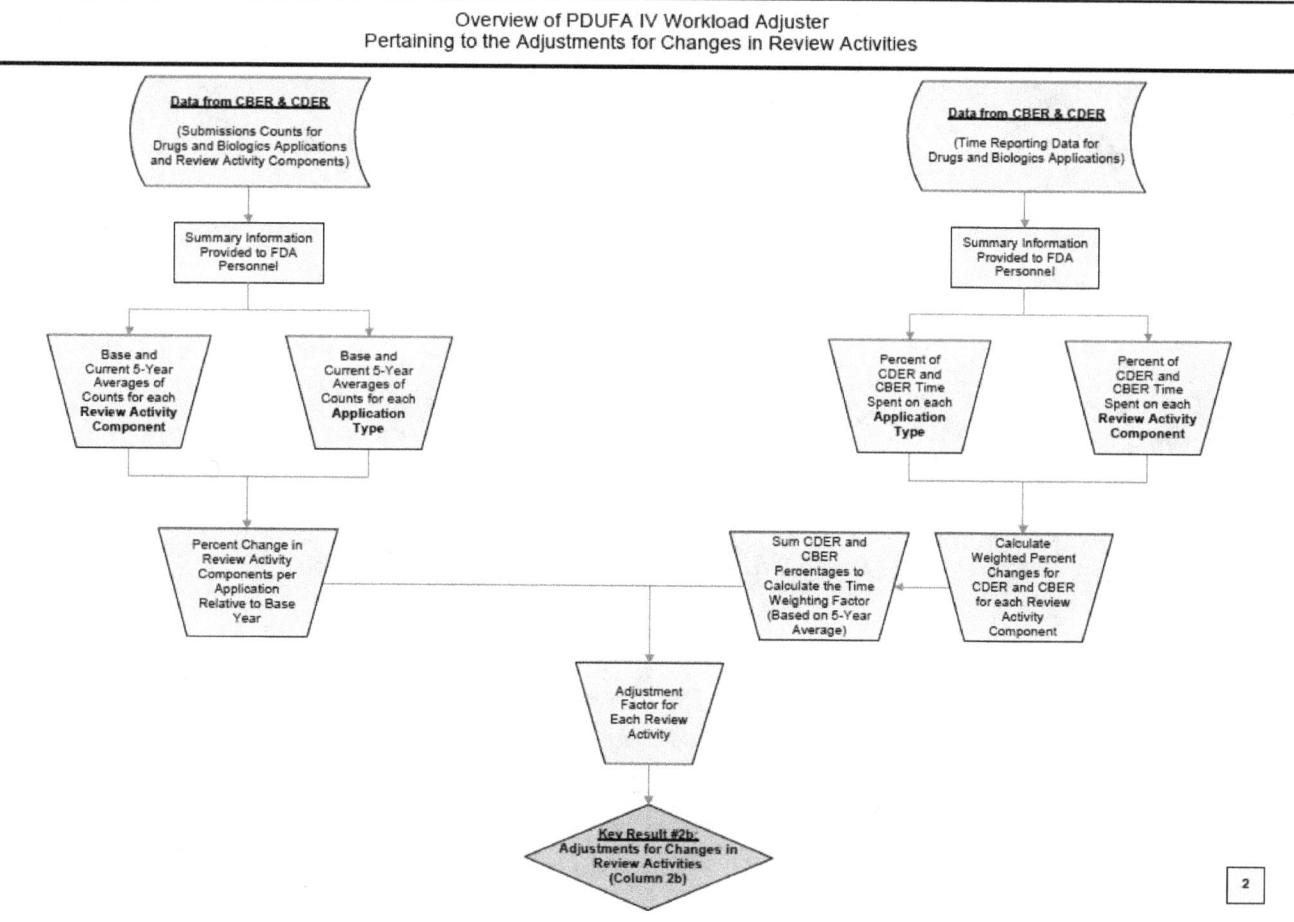

Overview of PDUFA IV Workload Adjuster
Pertaining to the Adjustments for Changes in Review Activities

2

Overview of PDUFA IV Workload Adjuster
Pertaining to the Adjustments for Changes in Review Activities

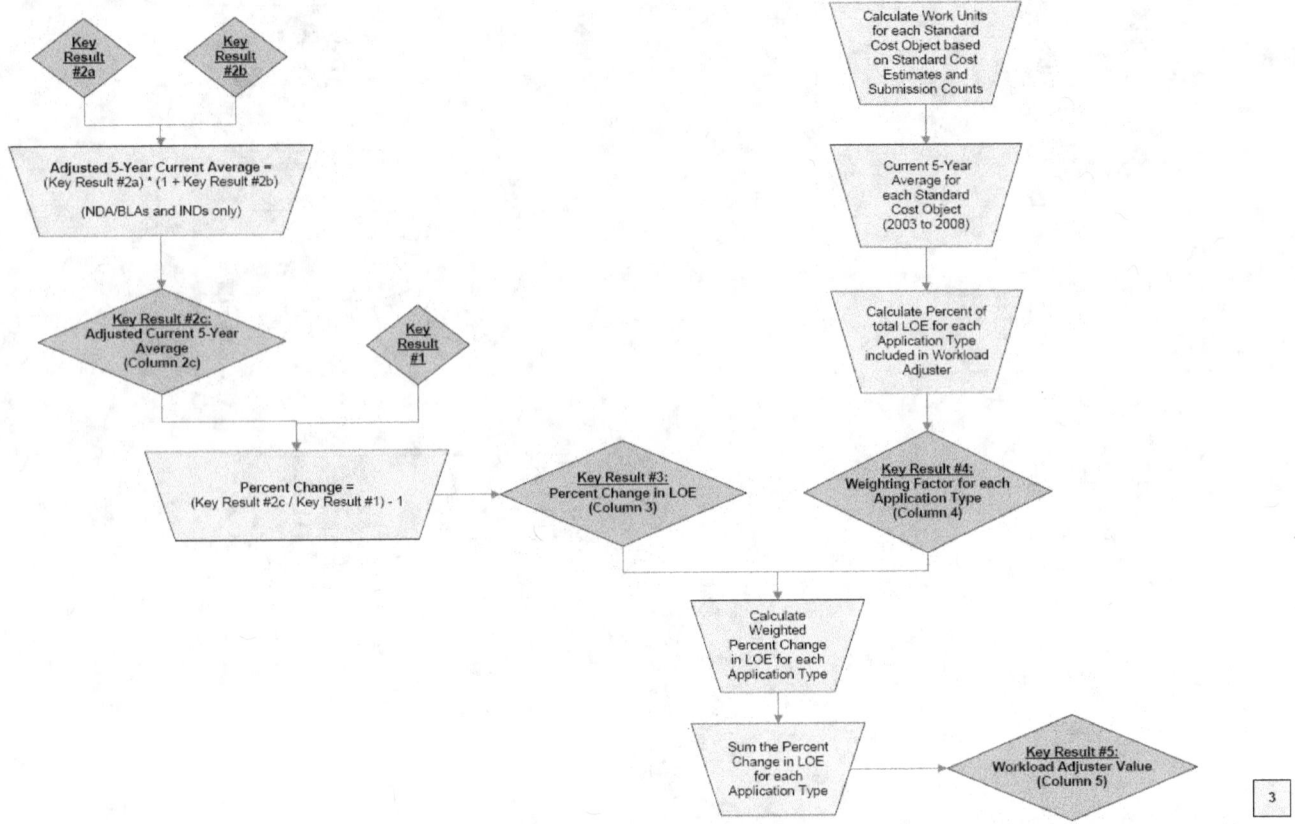

Appendix B: Supporting Information for Monte Carlo Analysis

The results of the linear regression analysis that was performed on the seven model inputs are presented in charts and table in Figures B1 through B7. (Note: The FY 2002 5-year average used by FDA covers four years and not five years due to the lack of data available for FY 1997.)

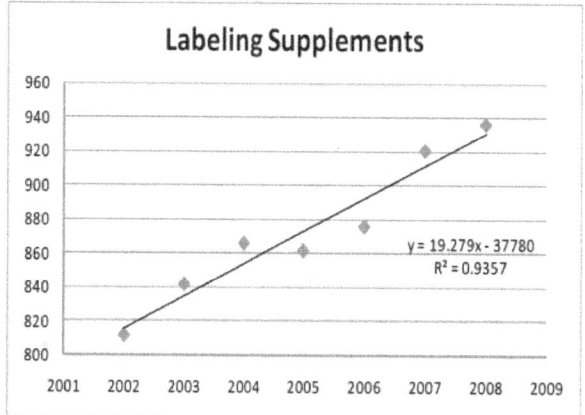

Labeling Supplements			
Fiscal Year	Regression	Data Point	Difference
2002	816.558	817.8	1.242
2003	835.837	811.8	-24.037
2004	855.116	841.8	-13.316
2005	874.395	866	-8.395
2006	893.674	861.6	-32.074
2007	912.953	876	-36.953
2008	932.232	920.4	-11.832
2009	951.511		
		Mean Difference:	-17.90928571
		Standard Deviation:	13.6392578

Figure B1 – Regression Analysis on Labeling Supplements

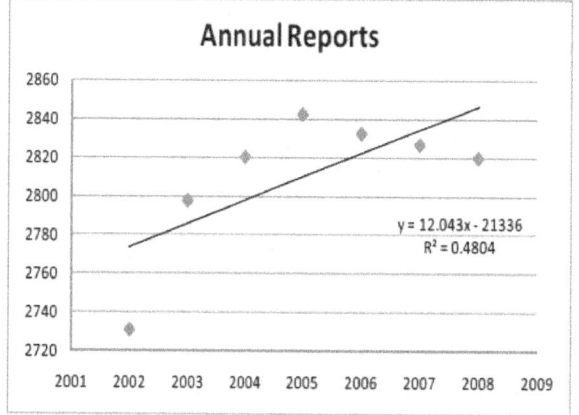

Annual Reports			
Fiscal Year	Regression	Data Point	Difference
2002	2774.086	2730.8	-43.286
2003	2786.129	2797.6	11.471
2004	2798.172	2820.2	22.028
2005	2810.215	2842.4	32.185
2006	2822.258	2832.4	10.142
2007	2834.301	2826.6	-7.701
2008	2846.344	2819.8	-26.544
2009	2858.387		
		Mean Difference:	-0.243571429
		Standard Deviation:	27.05766329

Figure B2 - Regression Analysis on Annual Reports

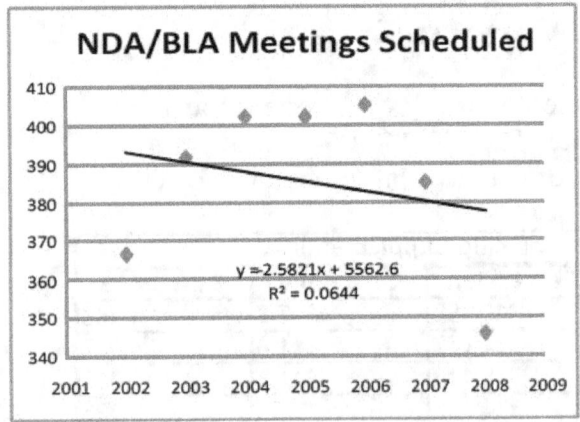

NDA/BLA Meetings Scheduled			
Fiscal Year	Regression	Data Point	Difference
2002	393.2358	366.5	-26.7358
2003	390.6537	391.6	0.9463
2004	388.0716	402	13.9284
2005	385.4895	402	16.5105
2006	382.9074	405	22.0926
2007	380.3253	385	4.6747
2008	377.7432	345.8	-31.9432
2009	375.1611		
		Mean Difference:	-0.075214286
		Standard Deviation:	21.26248513

Figure B3 – Regression Analysis on NDA/BLA Meetings Scheduled

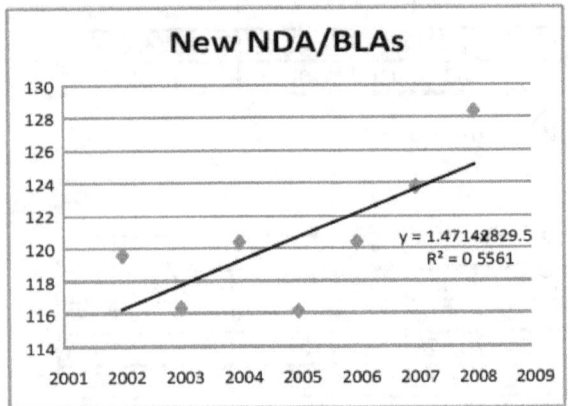

New NDA/BLAs			
Fiscal Year	Regression	Data Point	Difference
2002	116.2428	119.6	3.3572
2003	117.7142	116.4	-1.3142
2004	119.1856	120.4	1.2144
2005	120.657	116.2	-4.457
2006	122.1284	120.4	-1.7284
2007	123.5998	123.8	0.2002
2008	125.0712	128.4	3.3288
2009	126.5426		
		Mean Difference:	0.085857143
		Standard Deviation:	2.840020121

Figure B4 – Regression Analysis on NDA/BLA Applications

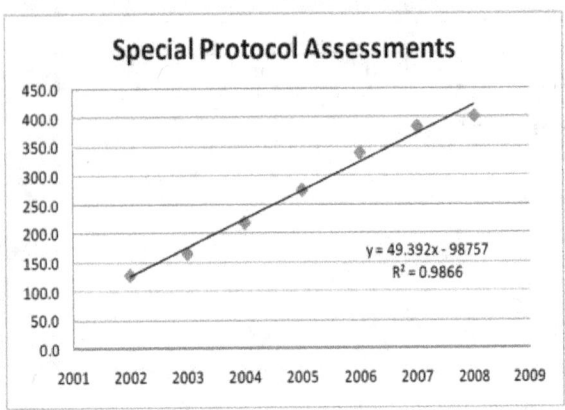

Special Protocol Assessments			
Fiscal Year	Regression	Data Point	Difference
2002	125.784	127.8	2.04933333
2003	175.176	165.1	-10.109333
2004	224.568	217.8	-6.768
2005	273.96	275.0	1.04
2006	323.352	339.0	15.648
2007	372.744	384.4	11.656
2008	422.136	402.2	-19.936
2009	471.528		
		Mean Difference:	-0.9171429
		Standard Deviation:	12.4201724

Figure B5 – Regression Analysis on SPAs

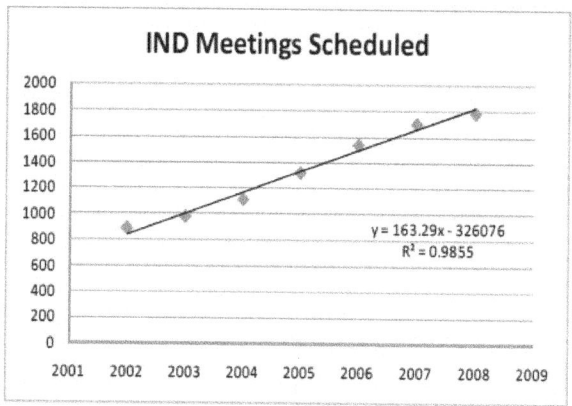

IND Meetings Scheduled			
Fiscal Year	Regression	Data Point	Difference
2002	830.58	885.3	54.67
2003	993.87	975.8	-18.07
2004	1157.16	1110.0	-47.16
2005	1320.45	1318.0	-2.45
2006	1483.74	1535.2	51.46
2007	1647.03	1699.4	52.37
2008	1810.32	1785.2	-25.12
2009	1973.61		
		Mean Difference:	9.385714286
		Standard Deviation:	42.72103965

Figure B6 - Regression Analysis on IND Meetings Scheduled

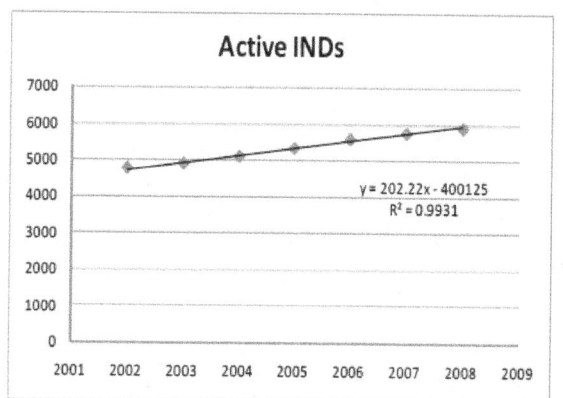

Active INDs			
Fiscal Year	Regression	Data Point	Difference
2002	4719.44	4751.8	32.36
2003	4921.66	4887.4	-34.26
2004	5123.88	5095.6	-28.28
2005	5326.1	5328.8	2.7
2006	5528.32	5582.6	55.28
2007	5730.54	5755.8	25.26
2008	5932.76	5897.6	-35.16
2009	6134.98		
		Mean Difference:	2.55714286
		Standard Deviation:	36.3142863

Figure B7 - Regression Analysis on IND Applications

The detailed results of the Monte Carlo simulations for both the baseline model (Figures B8 and B9) and alternative model (Figures B10 and B11) are presented below:

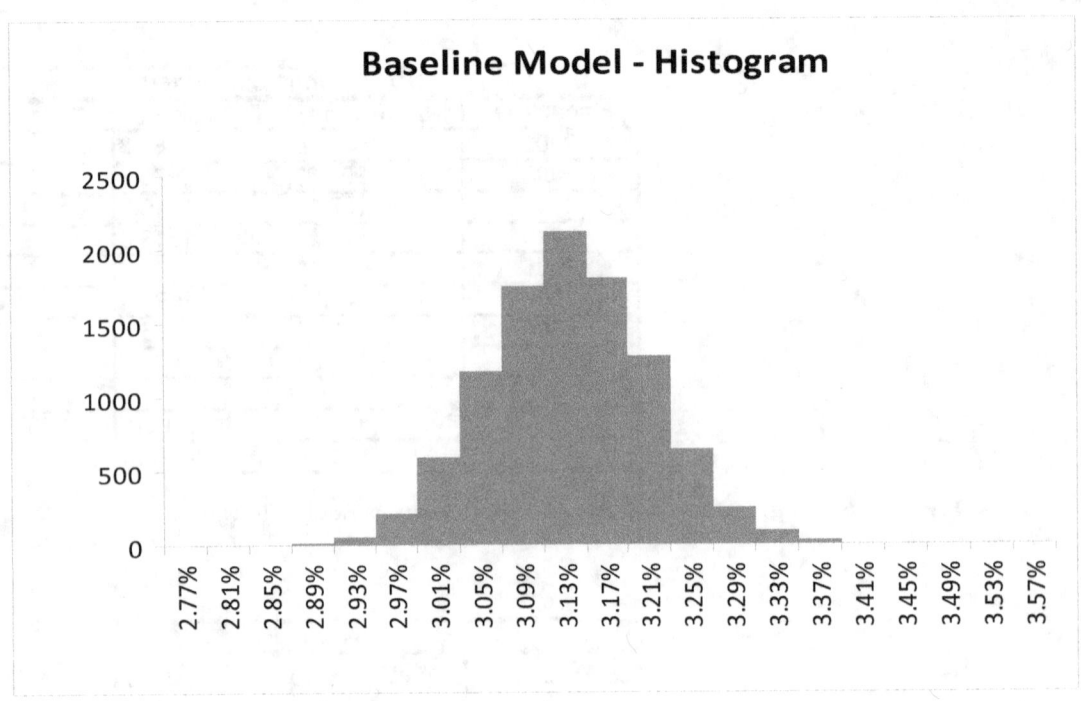

Figure B8 – Histogram of Monte Carlo Analysis Results for Baseline Model

Baseline Model - Details of Monte Carlo Analysis Results						
		Percentile Distribution		Histogram Data		Interval Probability Data	
Mean	**3.1137%**	Percentile	Value	Bin	Frequency	Value	Probability
Number of Trials	10,000	0%	2.81%	2.77%	0	2.77%	0.00%
		5%	2.99%	2.81%	0	2.81%	0.00%
		10%	3.02%	2.85%	3	2.85%	0.03%
Minimum	2.8115%	15%	3.03%	2.89%	14	2.89%	0.14%
Maximum	3.4933%	20%	3.05%	2.93%	49	2.93%	0.49%
Median	3.1133%	25%	3.06%	2.97%	212	2.97%	2.12%
Range	0.6819%	30%	3.07%	3.01%	591	3.01%	5.91%
		35%	3.08%	3.05%	1,175	3.05%	11.75%
Standard Deviation	**0.0766%**	40%	3.09%	3.09%	1,744	3.09%	17.44%
Variance	0.0001%	45%	3.10%	3.13%	2,112	3.13%	21.12%
		50%	3.11%	3.17%	1,801	3.17%	18.01%
Skewness	4.9092%	55%	3.12%	3.21%	1,278	3.21%	12.78%
Kurtosis	305.4457%	60%	3.13%	3.25%	646	3.25%	6.46%
		65%	3.14%	3.29%	254	3.29%	2.54%
		70%	3.15%	3.33%	93	3.33%	0.93%
		75%	3.17%	3.37%	21	3.37%	0.21%
		80%	3.18%	3.41%	6	3.41%	0.06%
		85%	3.19%	3.45%	0	3.45%	0.00%
		90%	3.21%	3.49%	0	3.49%	0.00%
		95%	3.24%	3.53%	1	3.53%	0.01%
		100%	3.49%	3.57%	0	3.57%	0.00%
	Total:				10,000		100.00%

Figure B9 – Details of Monte Carlo Analysis Results for Baseline Model

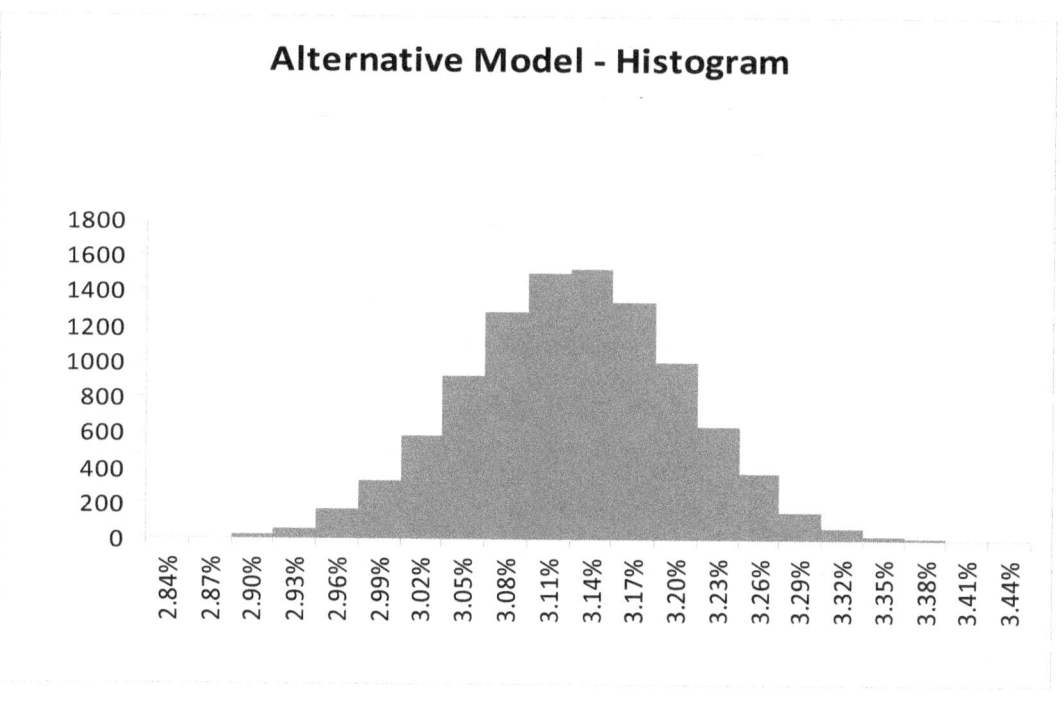

Figure B10 – Histogram of Monte Carlo Analysis Results for Alternative Model

Alternative Model - Details of Monte Carlo Analysis Results							
		Percentile Distribution		Histogram Data		Interval Probability Data	
Mean	3.1125%	Percentile	Value	Bin	Frequency	Value	Probability
Number of Trials	10,000	0%	2.82%	2.84%	2	2.84%	0.02%
		5%	2.99%	2.87%	3	2.87%	0.03%
		10%	3.01%	2.90%	24	2.90%	0.24%
Minimum	2.8156%	15%	3.03%	2.93%	53	2.93%	0.53%
Maximum	3.3889%	20%	3.05%	2.96%	164	2.96%	1.64%
Median	3.1126%	25%	3.06%	2.99%	324	2.99%	3.24%
Range	0.5734%	30%	3.07%	3.02%	583	3.02%	5.83%
		35%	3.08%	3.05%	925	3.05%	9.25%
Standard Deviation	0.0768%	40%	3.09%	3.08%	1,281	3.08%	12.81%
Variance	0.0001%	45%	3.10%	3.11%	1,499	3.11%	14.99%
		50%	3.11%	3.14%	1,527	3.14%	15.27%
Skewness	-0.8258%	55%	3.12%	3.17%	1,344	3.17%	13.44%
Kurtosis	299.3935%	60%	3.13%	3.20%	1,003	3.20%	10.03%
		65%	3.14%	3.23%	632	3.23%	6.32%
		70%	3.15%	3.26%	377	3.26%	3.77%
		75%	3.16%	3.29%	158	3.29%	1.58%
		80%	3.18%	3.32%	64	3.32%	0.64%
		85%	3.19%	3.35%	23	3.35%	0.23%
		90%	3.21%	3.38%	11	3.38%	0.11%
		95%	3.24%	3.41%	3	3.41%	0.03%
		100%	3.39%	3.44%	0	3.44%	0.00%
	Totals				10,000		100.00%

Figure B11 – Details of Monte Carlo Analysis Results for Alternative Model

Appendix C: Documents Provided by Client

The following represent the list of documents provided by FDA:

- Documents from PDUFA History Lesson Meeting

- Documents from CDER and CBER Time Reporting Briefings

- Federal Register notice as of 08-01-08

- Documents on original development of standard cost methodology from Arthur Andersen and KPMG reports

- The standard cost model workbook

- The PDUFA IV Workload Adjuster workbook

- The PDUFA III Simulation workbook

- List of Activity Codes from CDER Time Reporting System and CBER Resource Reporting System for PDUFA-related activities

- Article entitled "Test Tube to Patient"

- List of other review activities that were maintained and/or considered during the transition from PDUFA III to PDUFA IV

- FY 2007 Financial Report

- FY 2007 Performance Report

- CDER and CBER data from FY 1997 through FY 2005

- Data and clarification on the different types of meetings that occur during the PDUFA drug application review process

- Time reporting percentages for FY 2006 and FY 2007

- CDER submission counts and complexity factor data from FY 2002 through FY 2008

- CBER submission counts and complexity factor data from FY 2002 through FY 2008

Appendix D: Methodology for the Alternative Workload Adjuster with Weighted Time Reporting

1. First, calculate the total process costs for NDA/BLA and IND applications by adding together the standard process costs for the different types of NDAs/BLAs and active INDs for each fiscal year. The calculations were performed as follows:

   a. [A] = Total NDA/BLA Process Costs =

      (NDA NME with Clinical Data) +

      (NDA xNME with Clinical Data) +

      (NDA xNME without Clinical Data) +

      (BLAs reviewed by CDER) +

      (BLAs reviewed by CBER)

   b. [B] = Total IND Process Costs =

      (Drug INDs) +

      (Biologic INDs reviewed by CDER) +

      (Biologic INDs reviewed by CBER)

2. Second, multiply the total NDA/BLA and IND process costs by the corresponding time weighting factor (already provided) to generate the weighted process costs for each review activity. The calculations for each review activity component were performed as follows, for each fiscal year for which data is available:

   a. [C] = Labeling Supplements Weighted Process Costs =

      [A] * (Time Weighting Factor for Labeling Supplements)

   b. [D] = Annual Reports Weighted Process Costs =

      [A] * (Time Weighting Factor for Annual Reports)

   c. [E] = NDA/BLA Meetings Scheduled =

      [A] * (Time Weighting Factor for NDA/BLA Meetings Scheduled)

   d. [F] = SPAs Weighted Process Costs =

      [B] * (Time Weighing Factor for SPAs)

   e. [G] = IND Meetings Scheduled =

      [B] * (Time Weighting Factor for IND Meetings Scheduled)

3. Third, calculate the current 5-year average of the weighed process costs. The calculations were performed as follows:

a. Labeling Supplements Weighted Time Reporting Percentage =

(Current 5-Year Average of [C]) / (Current 5-Year Average of [A])

b. Annual Reports Weighted Time Reporting Percentage =

([(Current 5-Year Average of [D]) / (Current 5-Year Average of [A])

c. NDA/BLA Meetings Scheduled Weighted Time Reporting Percentage =

(Current 5-Year Average of [E]) / (Current 5-Year Average of [A])

d. SPAs Weighted Time Reporting Percentage =

(Current 5-Year Average of [F]) / (Current 5-Year Average of [B])

e. IND Meetings Scheduled Weighted Time Reporting Percentage =

(Current 5-Year Average of [G]) / (Current 5-Year Average of [B])

Once the process cost weighted time reporting percentages are calculated for each review activity component, the remaining calculations are performed according to the current methodology. (i.e., the adjustments for changes in review activities are still a sum of the individual activity factors as described above).

Glossary

Abbreviated New Drug Applications (ANDA) – Applications submitted for generic drug products that are comparable to an innovator drug product in dosage form, strength, route of administration, quality, performance characteristics and intended use. The review of ANDAs is not a part of the process for the review of human drug applications as defined in PDUFA.

Annual Reports – A report submitted annually by the applicant within 60 days of the anniversary date of U.S. approval of the application.

Biologics License Applications (BLA) – A biologics license application is a submission that contains specific information on the manufacturing processes, chemistry, pharmacology, clinical pharmacology and the medical affects of the biologic product. If the information provided meets FDA requirements, the application is approved and a license is issued allowing the firm to market the product.

Efficacy Supplements – Following approval of an original NDA or BLA, a sponsor may later submit an application to expand the disease indications included in the drug labeling. This application often includes additional clinical study data to support the proposed change in labeling, and is referred to as an Efficacy Supplement. FDA's review of Efficacy Supplements is very similar to the review of original NDAs and BLAs, and results in an action letter to the sponsor outlining FDA's decision.

Investigational New Drug Applications (IND) – An Investigational New Drug Application (IND) is a request for Food and Drug Administration (FDA) authorization to administer an investigational drug to humans. Such authorization must be secured prior to interstate shipment and administration of any new drug that is not the subject of an approved new drug application.

Labeling Supplements – The sponsor of an approved drug may submit a labeling supplement for human prescription drugs and biological products to change the pertinent information about the appropriate use of the drugs or biological products.

Manufacturing Supplements – The details of manufacturing are described in the Chemistry and Manufacturing Controls (CMC) section of the NDA. After product approval, sponsors often continue to refine the manufacturing process. They must submit these changes in a manufacturing supplement for FDA review, and await FDA prior approval before implementing more significant changes proposed in CMC supplements.

New Drug Applications (NDA) – When the sponsor of a new drug believes that enough evidence on the drug's safety and effectiveness has been obtained to meet FDA's requirements for marketing approval, the sponsor submits to FDA a new drug application (NDA). The application must contain data from specific technical viewpoints for review, including chemistry, pharmacology, medical, biopharmaceutics, and statistics. If the NDA is approved, the product may be marketed in the United States.

New Molecular Entity (NME) – A New Molecular Entity is an active ingredient that has never before been marketed in the United States in any form.

Prescription Drug User Fee Act (PDUFA) – In 1992, Congress passed the Prescription Drug User Fee Act (PDUFA). PDUFA authorized FDA to collect fees from companies that produce certain human drug and biological products. Any time a company wants the FDA to approve a new drug or biologic prior to marketing it must submit an application along with a fee to support the review process. In addition, companies pay annual fees for each manufacturing establishment and for each prescription drug product marketed.
(http://www.fda.gov/ForIndustry/UserFees/PrescriptionDrugUserFee/ucm118833.htm)

Special Protocol Assessments (SPA) – The FDA reviews the SPAs submitted by sponsors to assess whether they are adequate to meet scientific and regulatory requirements identified by the sponsors. Three types of protocols related to PDUFA products are eligible for this special protocol assessment under the PDUFA goals: Animal Carcinogenicity protocols; Final Product Stability protocols; and Clinical protocols.